NEXT MOVE 5

Student's Book

Amanda Cant and Mary Charrington

MACMILLAN

Contents

Key

Write / Number

Color

Circle / Draw

Match / Follow

Point

Say

Sing

Count

Act

Play

Make

Listen

World music

Me
Activities that develop social and creative skills and foster intrapersonal intelligence

Think
Activities that develop critical thinking skills in identifying, processing, and manipulating information

Learn
Activities that build learner autonomy and promote the use of learning strategies

Collaborate / Communicate
Activities that develop collaborative skills through teamwork and effective communication

Act
Activities that create societal understanding by promoting tolerance and ethical behavior

The World

Track 2 CD 1 Sing the song.

Unit 1

Workbook page 3

Track 3

1 Listen and point.

Track 4

2 Listen and match.

Workbook page 4

Grammar I'm (Roberto).

Track 5

1 Listen and point.

1

2

2 Say *Hello* and *Goodbye.*

Workbook page 5

Unit 1 Lesson 3

Track 6

1 Listen and say.

Track 7

2 Listen and play.

Workbook page 6

Lesson 4

Track 8

1 Listen and say.

1 2 3 4 5

6 7 8 9 10

Track 9

2 Sing and act out.

Workbook page 7

My Picture Dictionary page 106

Unit 1

Lesson 5

Grammar I'm (six).

Track 10

1 Listen and point.

2 Follow and say.

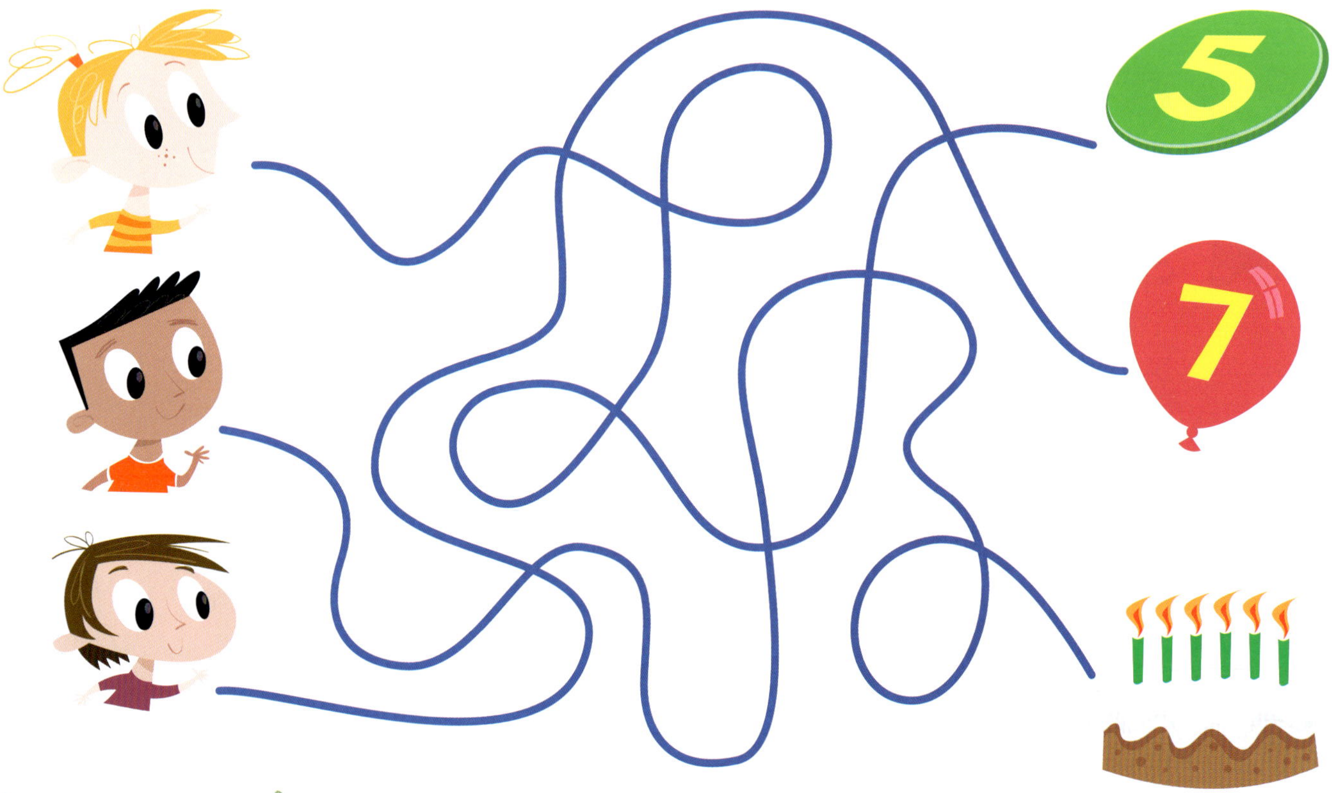

Workbook page 8

Lesson 6

1 Match and color.

9

2

3

7

5

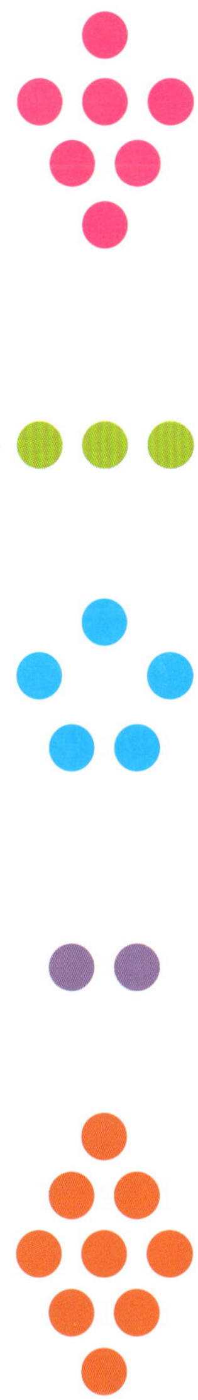

2 Write and say.

__ 2 3 4 __ 6 __ 8 __ 10

Workbook page 9

Unit 1 Lesson 7

Story Time

Track 11

1 Listen and point.

2 Act out.

3 Circle the value.

Say **Hello** to your friends.

Workbook page 10

Craft Time

1 Make a people chain.

2 Show and say.

Workbook page 83

1 Say and color.

Track 12

2 Listen and number.

Korea

Track 13

Sing the song.

Unit 2

Workbook page 11

Track 14

1 Listen and point.

Track 15

2 Listen and number.

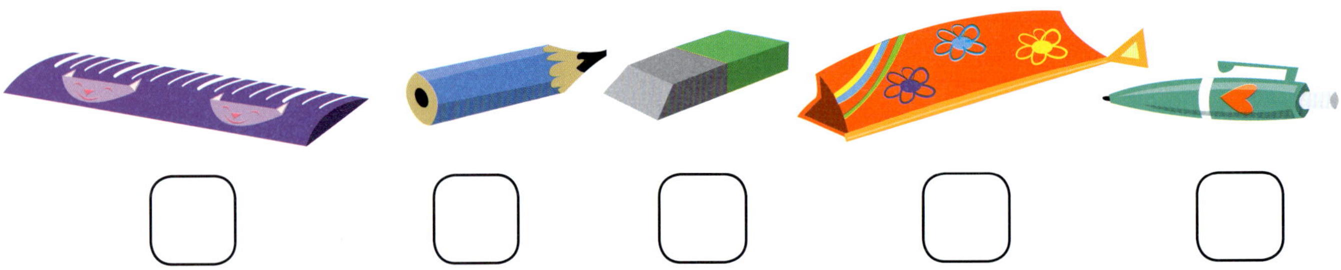

Workbook page 12

Grammar It's a (pencil).
It's an (eraser).

Track 16

1 Listen and point.

1

2

3

2 Draw and say.

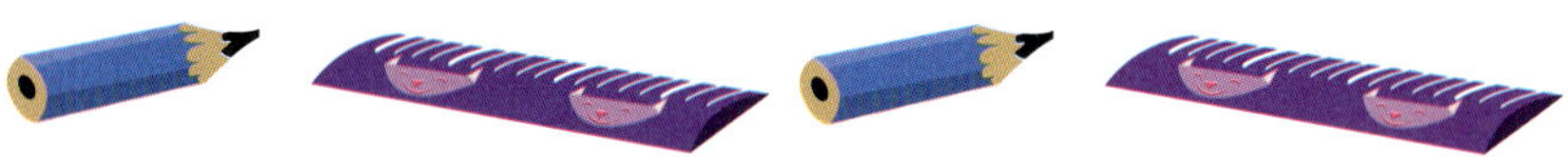

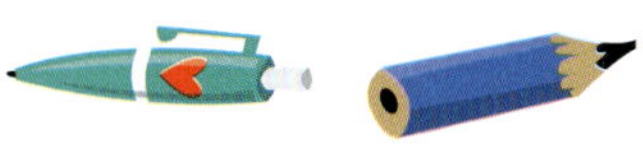

Workbook page 13

Unit 2 Lesson 3

1 Match and say.

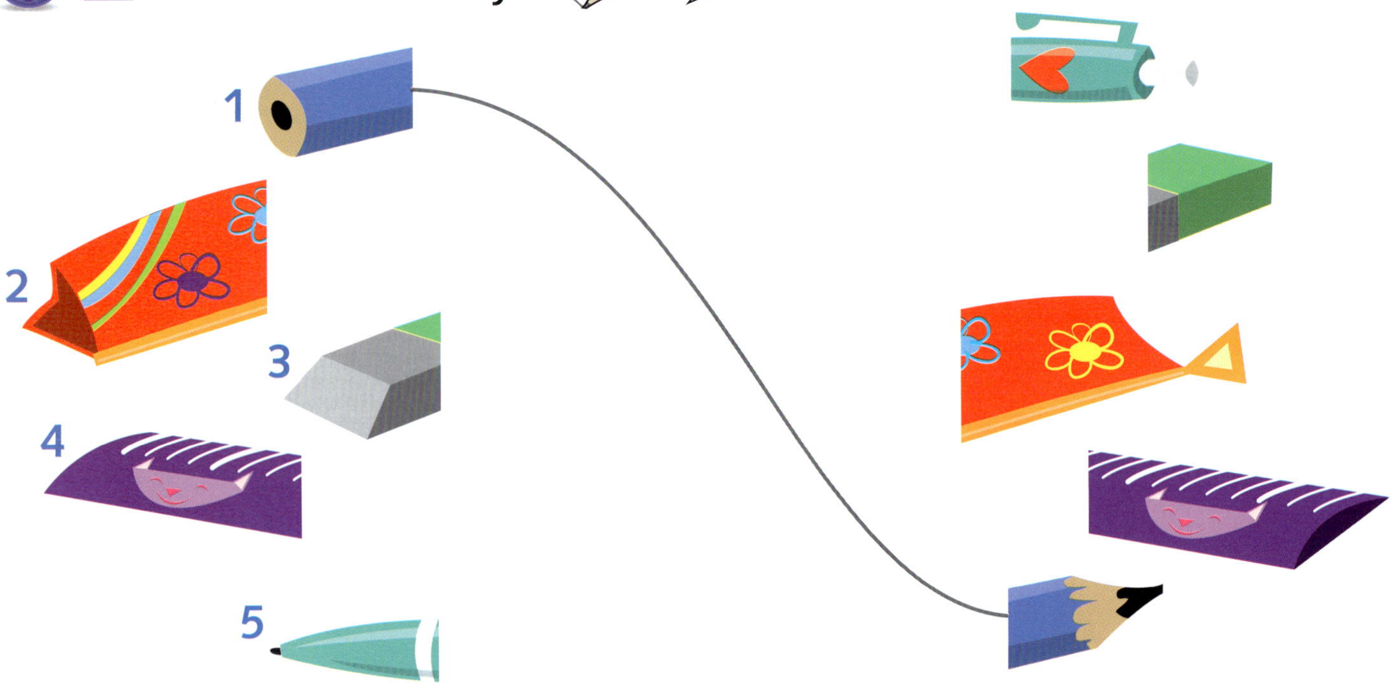

2 Play and say.

Workbook page 14

Lesson 4

Track 17

1 Listen and point.

Track 18

2 Sing and act out.

Workbook page 15

My Picture Dictionary page 106

Lesson 5

Grammar one book
two books

Track 19

1 Listen and point.

2 Play and say.

Workbook page 16

Lesson 6

1 Count and write.

2 Say.

Workbook page 17

Story Time

Track 20

1 Listen and point.

2 Act out.

3 Circle the value.

Take care of your school things.

Workbook page 18

Craft Time

1 Make pencil puppets.

2 Act out the story.

Workbook page 85

Progress Check

1 Say and color.

Track 21

2 Listen and number.

Brazil

Track 22

Sing the song.

Unit 3

Workbook page 19

Track 23

1 Listen and point.

Track 24

2 Listen and color.

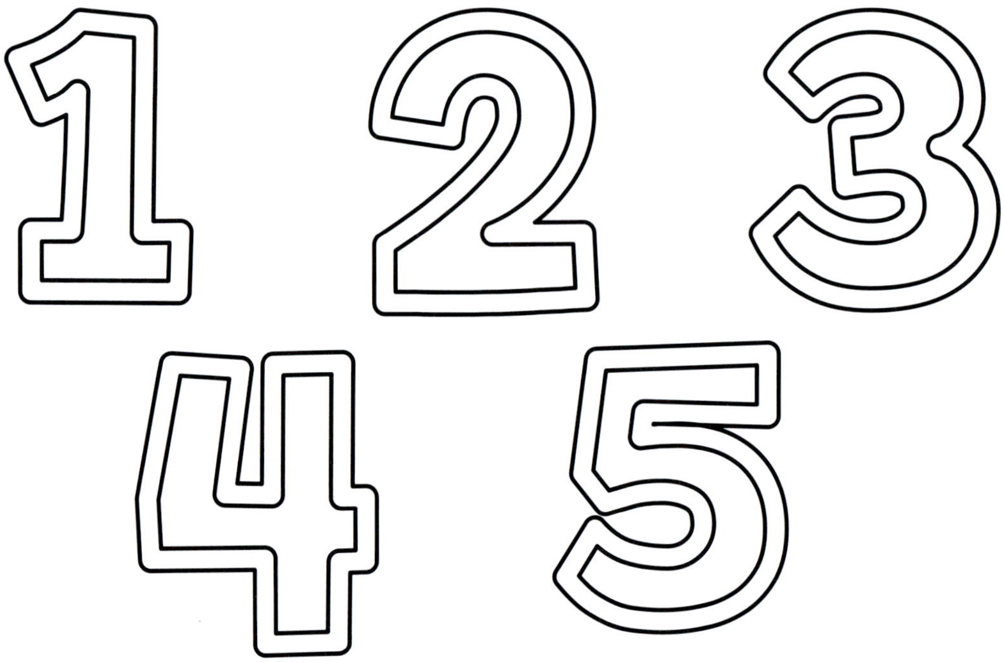

Workbook page 20

Grammar It's (red).

Track 25

1 Listen and point.

1

2

2 Circle and say.

Workbook page 21

1 Color.

1 2 3 4 5

2 Listen and point.

Track 26

Workbook page 22

Lesson 4

Track 27

1 Listen and point.

1 2 3 4 5

Track 28

2 Listen and color.

1 2 3 4 5

Track 29

3 Sing and act out.

Workbook page 23

My Picture Dictionary page 107

Grammar My (pencil) is (pink).

Track 30

1 Listen and point.

1

2

2 Play and say.

Workbook page 24

1 Follow and color.

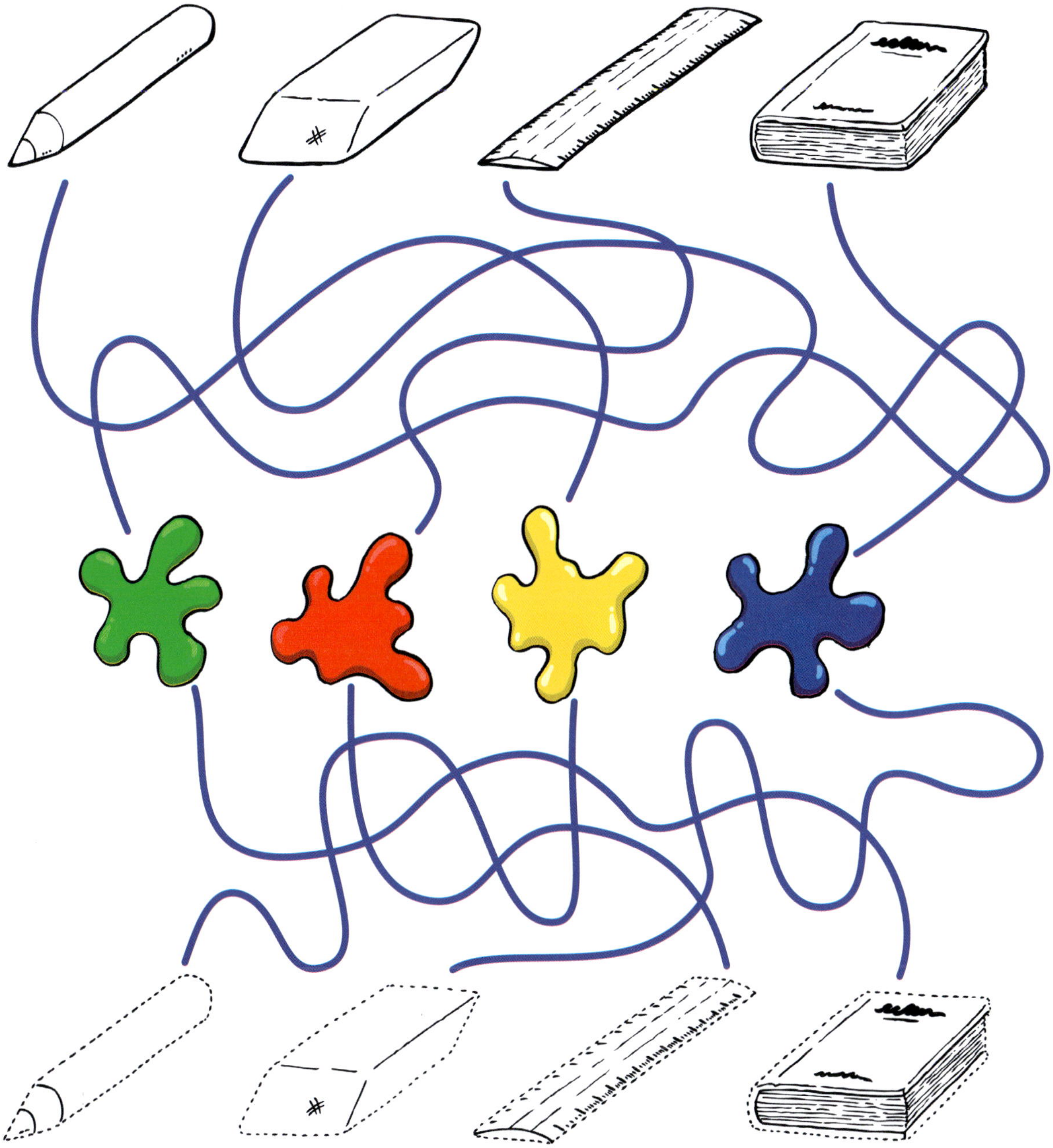

2 Play a game.

Workbook page 25

Story Time

Track 31

1 Listen and point.

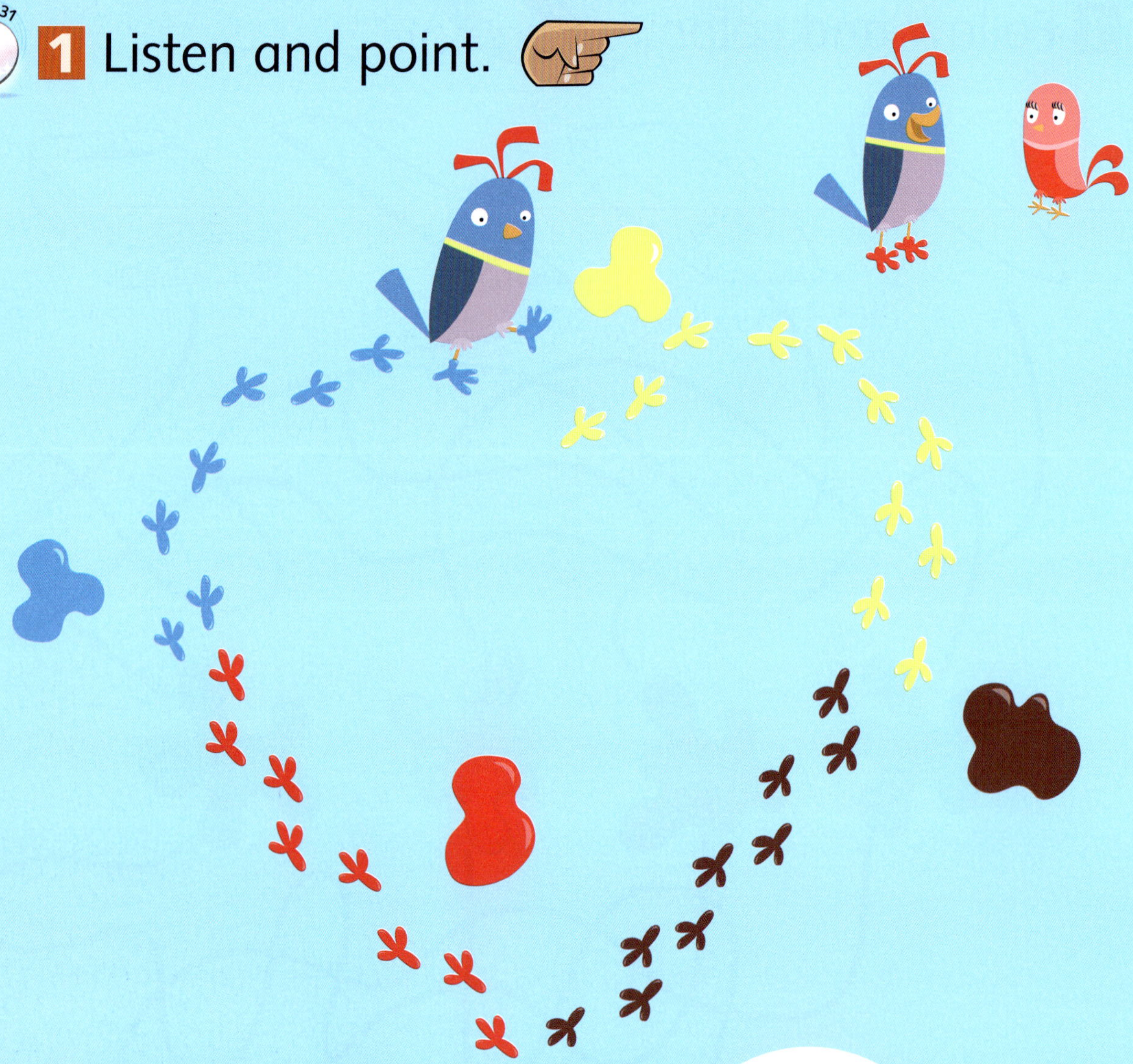

2 Act out.

3 Circle the value.

Express your opinions.

Workbook page 26

Craft Time

1 Make a heart.

2 Say.

Progress Check

1 Say and color.

Track 32

2 Listen and number.

Mexico

Track 33

Sing the song.

Unit 4

Workbook page 27

Story Time

Track 44

1 Listen and point.

2 Act out.

3 Circle the value.

Play together.

Workbook page 34

Craft Time

1 Draw a toy.

2 Play and say.

Progress Check

1 Say and color.

Track 45

2 Listen and number.

Ireland

Track 46 Sing the song.

Unit 5

Workbook page 35

Track 47

1 Listen and point.

Track 48

2 Listen and draw.

Workbook page 36

Grammar This is my (head).
These are my (arms).

Track 49

1 Listen and say.

1

2

3

Track 50

2 Listen and circle.

Workbook page 37

Track 51

1 Listen and color.

2 Act out and say.

Workbook page 38

Track 52

1 Listen and point.

Track 53

2 Sing and act out.

Workbook page 39

My Picture Dictionary page 108

Unit 5 Lesson 5

Grammar I have (a nose).
I have (two eyes).

Track 54

1 Listen and draw.

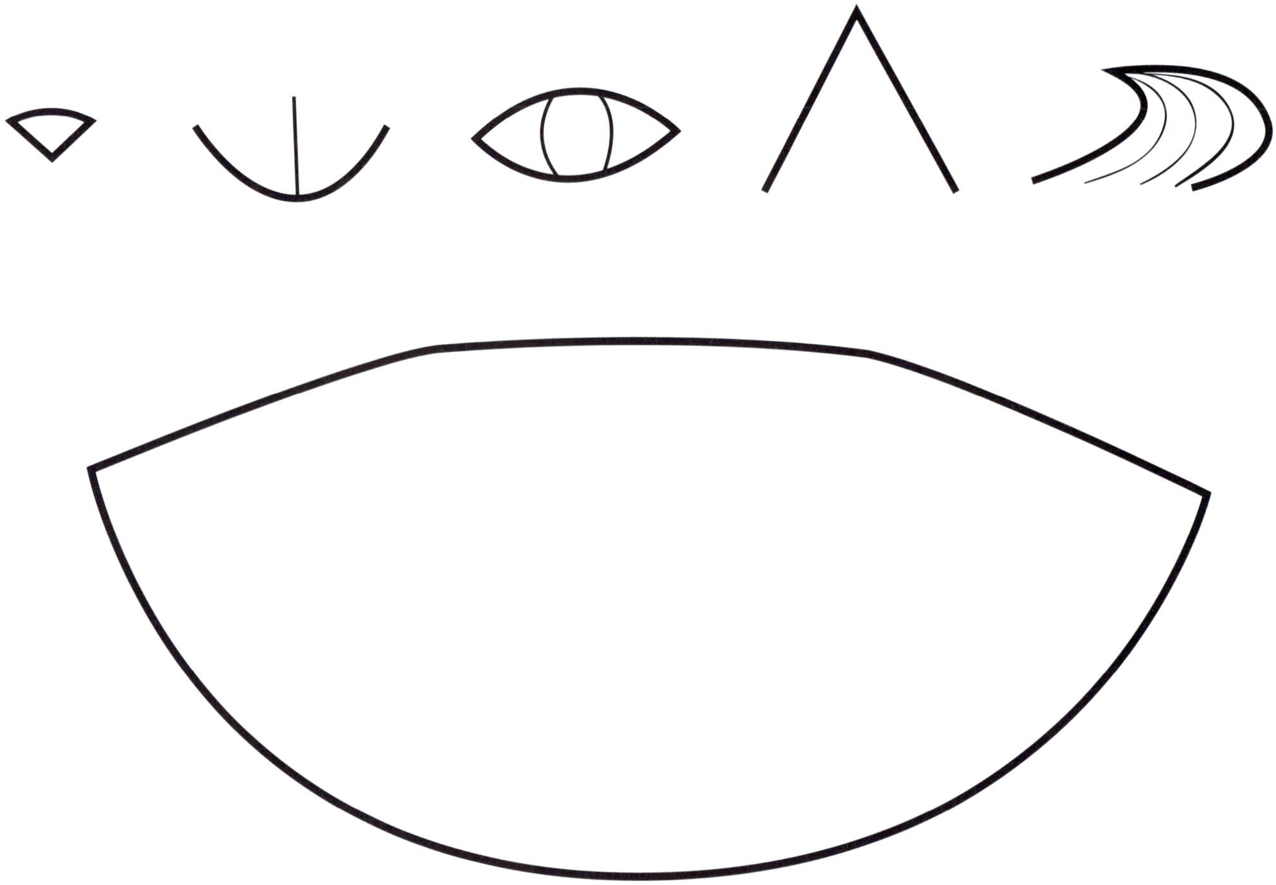

Track 55

2 Listen and say *Yes* or *No*.

1 2 3 4

Workbook page 40

Lesson 6

Track 56

1 Listen and match.

2 Act out and say.

Workbook page 41

Story Time

Track 57

1 Listen and point.

2 Act out.

3 Circle the value.

Help your friends.

Workbook page 42

Craft Time

1 Make a scarecrow.

2 Tell the story.

Workbook page 87

Progress Check

1 Say and color.

Track 58

2 Listen and number.

Vietnam

Track 2 CD 2 Sing the song.

Unit 6

Workbook page 43

Track 3

1 Listen and point.

2 Match and say.

sister

Workbook page 44

Grammar This is my (mom).

Track 4

1 Listen and point.

1

2

Track 5

2 Listen and match.

1

2

3

Workbook page 45

Unit 6 Lesson 7

Story Time

Track 11

1 Listen and point.

2 Act out.

3 Circle the value.

Help your family.

Workbook page 50

Grammar This is my (mom).

Track 4

1 Listen and point.

1

2

Track 5

2 Listen and match.

1

2

3

Workbook page 45

1 Draw your family.

2 Show and say.

Workbook page 46

Lesson 4

Track 6

1 Listen and point.

Track 7

2 Sing and act out.

Workbook page 47

My Picture Dictionary page 108

Lesson 5

Grammar My (grandma) is (old).

Track 8

1 Listen and point.

Track 9

2 Listen and circle.

Workbook page 48

Unit 6 Lesson 6

Track 10

1 Listen and circle.

2 Say and act out.

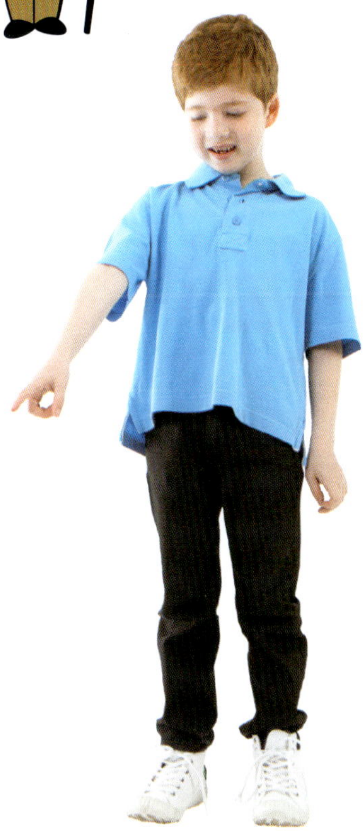

Workbook page 49

Unit 6 Lesson 7

Story Time

Track 11

1 Listen and point.

2 Act out.

3 Circle the value.

Help your family.

Workbook page 50

Craft Time

1 Make a family poster.

2 Show and say.

1 Say and color.

Track 12

2 Listen and number.

Botswana

Track 13

Sing the song.

Unit 7

Workbook page 51

Track 14

1 Listen and point.

2 Match and say.

Workbook page 52

Grammar It's (brown) and (yellow).

Track 15

1 Listen and point.

1

2

Track 16

2 Listen and color.

1

2

3

4

5

Workbook page 53

Unit 7 Lesson 7

Story Time

Track 21

1 Listen and point.

2 Act out.

3 Circle the value.

Respect other people's things.

Workbook page 58

Grammar It's (brown) and (yellow).

Track 15

1 Listen and point.

Track 16

2 Listen and color.

Workbook page 53

Unit 7 Lesson 3

Track 17

1 Listen and number.

2 Draw and say.

Workbook page 54

Track 18

1 Listen and point.

Track 19

2 Match and sing.

Workbook page 55

My Picture Dictionary page 109

Unit 7

Lesson 5

Grammar They're (hens).

Track 20

1 Listen and match.

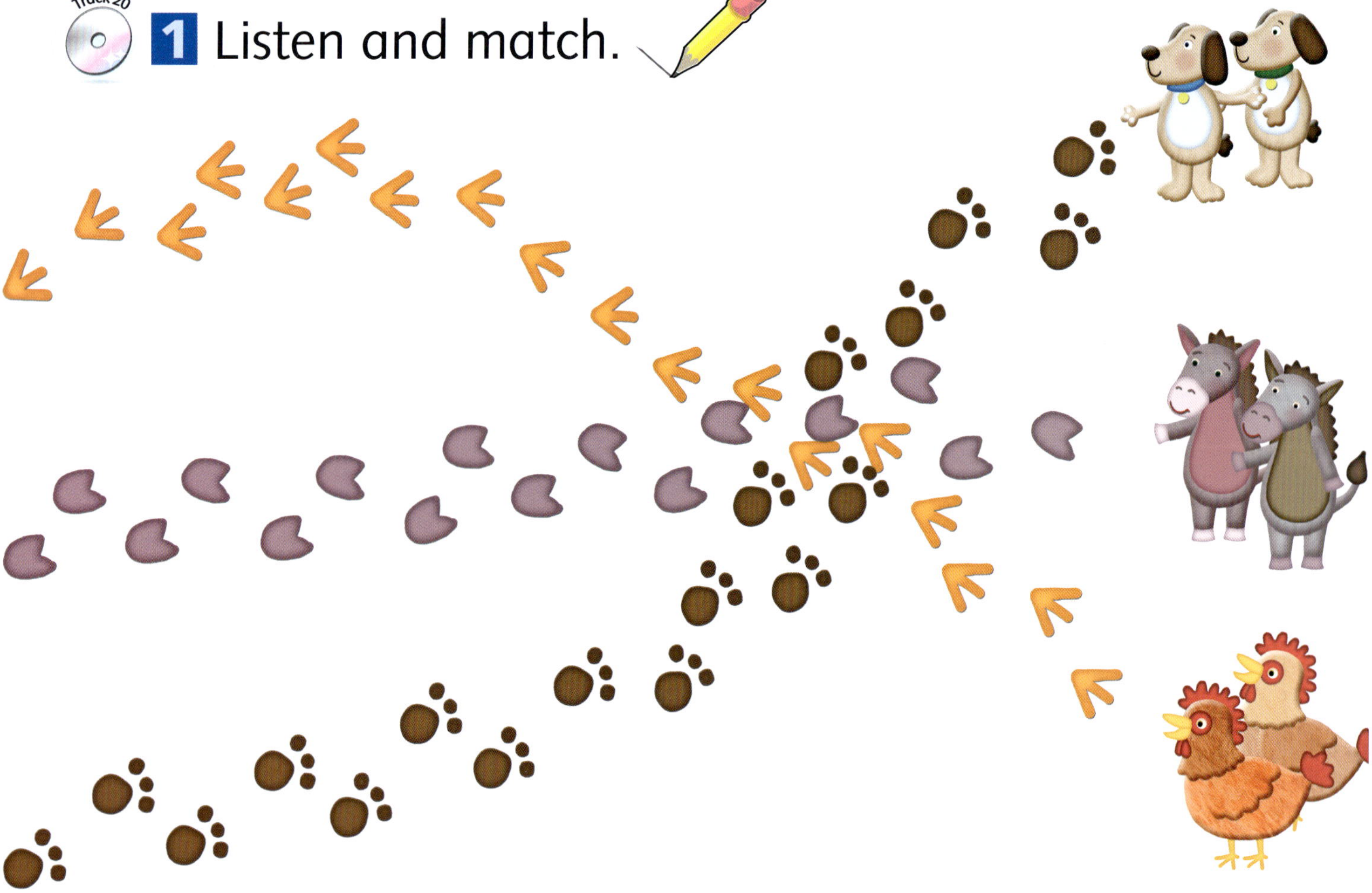

2 Match and say.

Workbook page 56

Unit 7 Lesson 6

1 Draw and say.

Workbook page 57

Story Time

Track 21

1 Listen and point.

2 Act out.

3 Circle the value.

Respect other people's things.

Workbook page 58

Craft Time

1 Make a goat.

2 Act out the story.

Workbook page 89

Progress Check

1 Say and color.

Track 22

2 Listen and number.

Peru

Sing the song.

Unit 8

Workbook page 59

Track 24

1 Listen and point.

2 Draw and say.

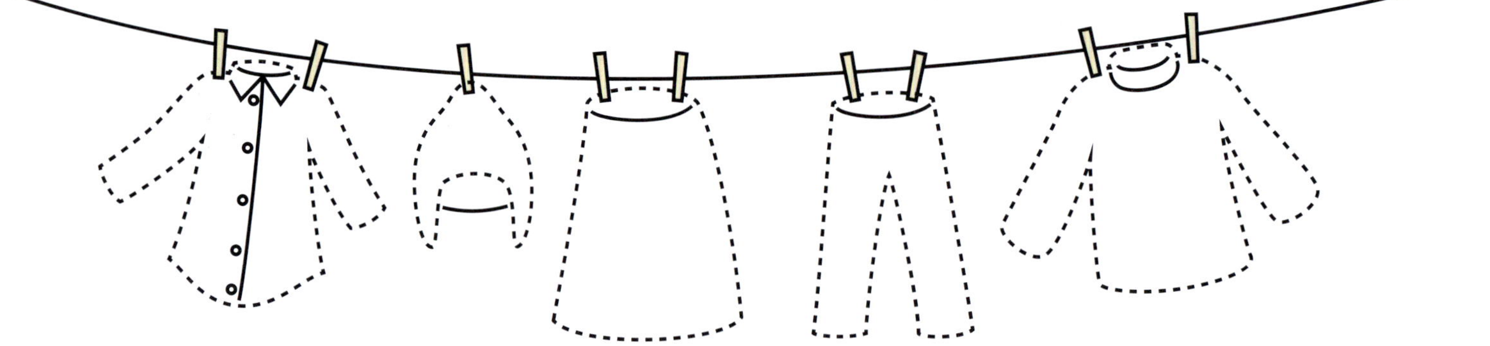

Workbook page 60

Unit 8 Lesson 2

Grammar It's my (hat).
They're my (pants).

Track 25

1 Listen and point.

1

2

Track 26

2 Listen and match.

1

2

Workbook page 61

1 Color.

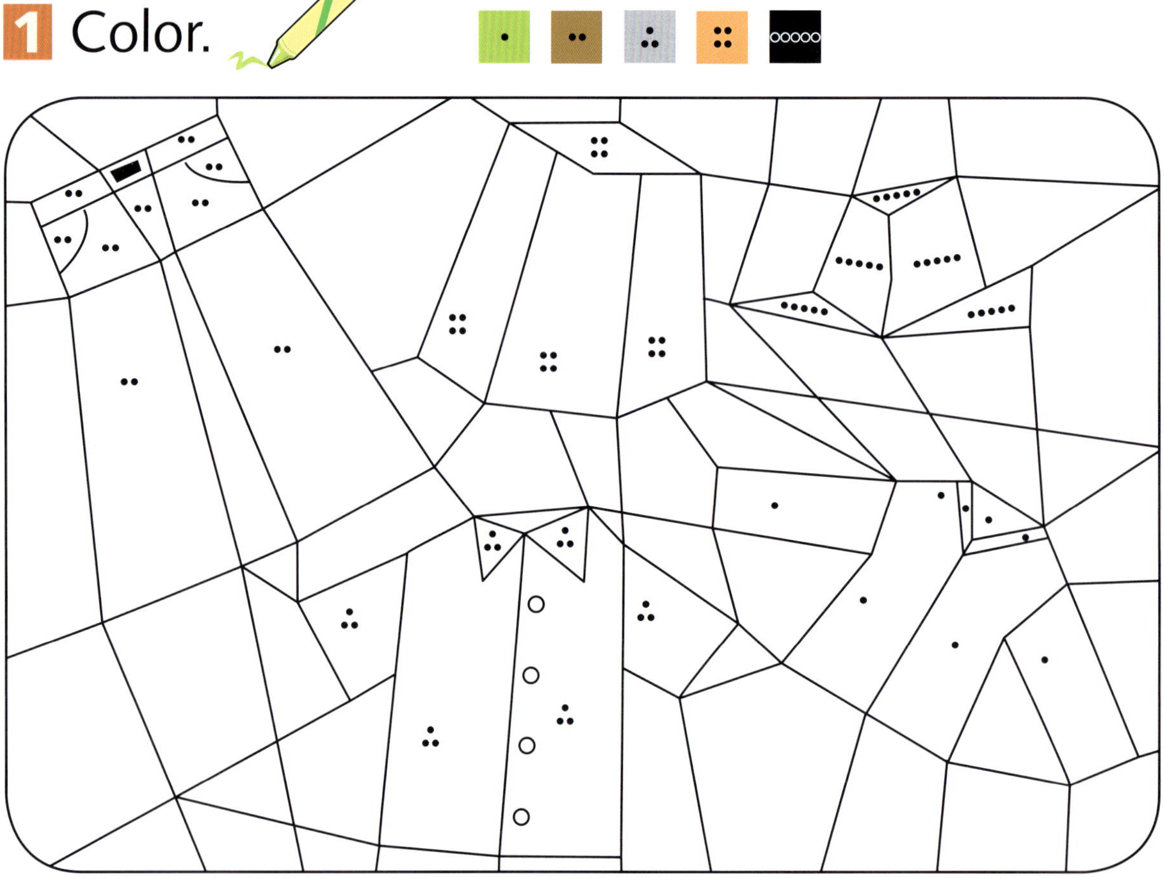

2 Act out and say.

Workbook page 62

Unit 8 Lesson 4

Track 27

1 Listen and point.

Track 28

2 Sing and act out.

Workbook page 63

My Picture Dictionary page 109

Unit 8 Lesson 5

Grammar It's your (hat).
They're your (shoes).

Track 29

1 Listen and point.

2 Circle and say.

Workbook page 64

Lesson 6

1 Circle and say.

2 Draw and say.

Workbook page 65

Story Time

Track 30

1 Listen and point.

2 Act out.

3 Circle the value.

Be sensible. Wear the right clothes.

Workbook page 66

Craft Time

1 Color and make.

2 Show and say.

Workbook page 91

Progress Check

1 Say and color.

Track 31

2 Listen and number.

Italy

Track 32

Sing the song.

Unit 9

Workbook page 67

Track 33

1 Listen and point.

2 Color and say.

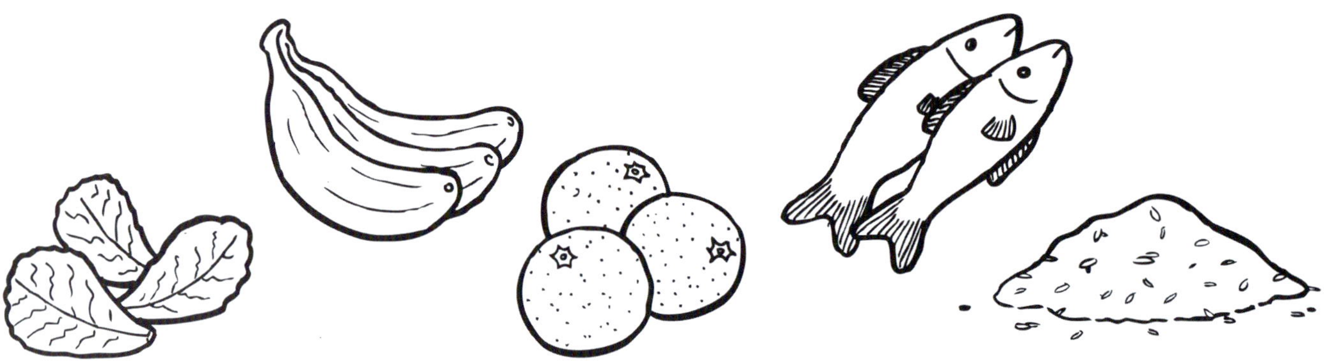

Workbook page 68

Grammar I like (salad).
I don't like (fish).

Track 34

1 Listen and point.

1

2

Track 35

2 Listen and draw ☺ or ☹.

1

2

3

4

5

Workbook page 69

1 Follow and say.

2 Say.

Workbook page 70

Track 36

1 Listen and point.

Track 37

2 Sing and act out.

Workbook page 71

My Picture Dictionary page 110

Unit 9 Lesson 5

Grammar Do you like (pasta)?
Yes, I do. / No, I don't

Track 38

1 Listen and point.

Track 39

2 Listen and say.

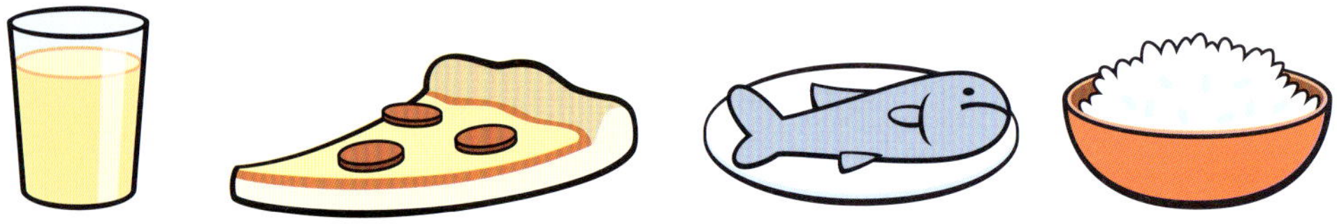

Workbook page 72

Track 40

1 Listen and draw 🙂 or ☹️.

2 Tell a friend.

Workbook page 73

Story Time

Track 41

1 Listen and point.

2 Act out.

3 Circle the value.

Be polite. Say **Please** and **Thank you.**

Workbook page 74

Craft Time

1 Make a pizza.

2 Play and say.

Progress Check

1 Say and color.

Track 42

2 Listen and number.

USA

Track 43

Sing the song.

Unit 10

Workbook page 75

1 Listen and point.

Track 44

2 Listen and match.

Track 45

Workbook page 76

Grammar I'm in the (bedroom).

Track 46

1 Listen and point.

1 2

Track 47

2 Listen and match.

1

2

3

4

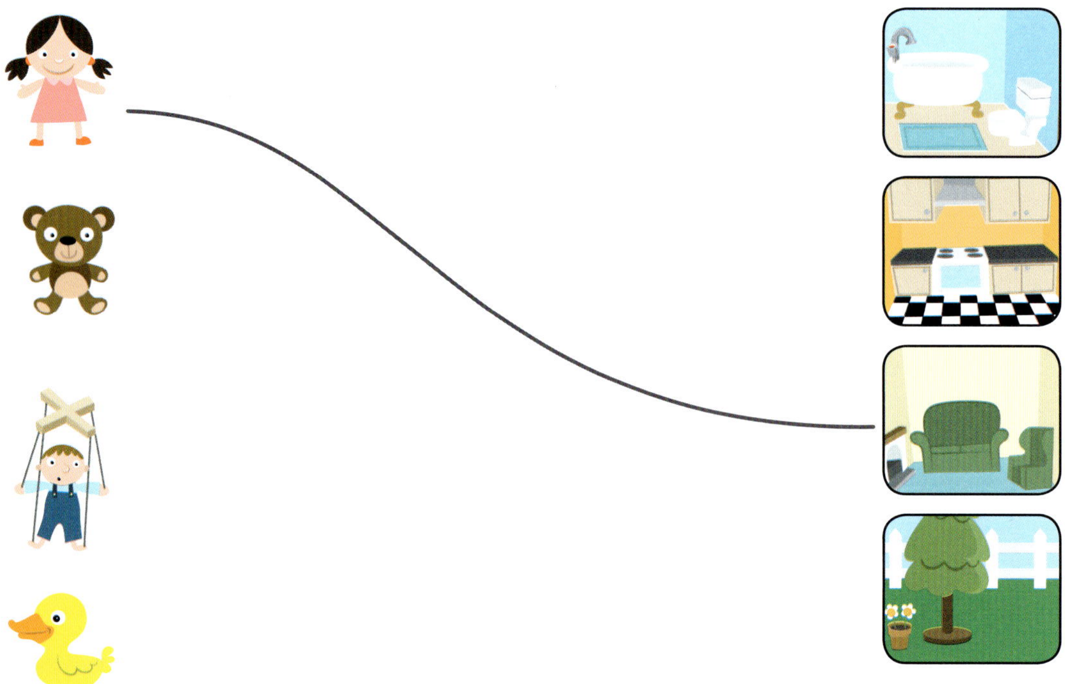

Track 48

3 Listen and say.

Workbook page 77

Track 49

1 Listen and draw.

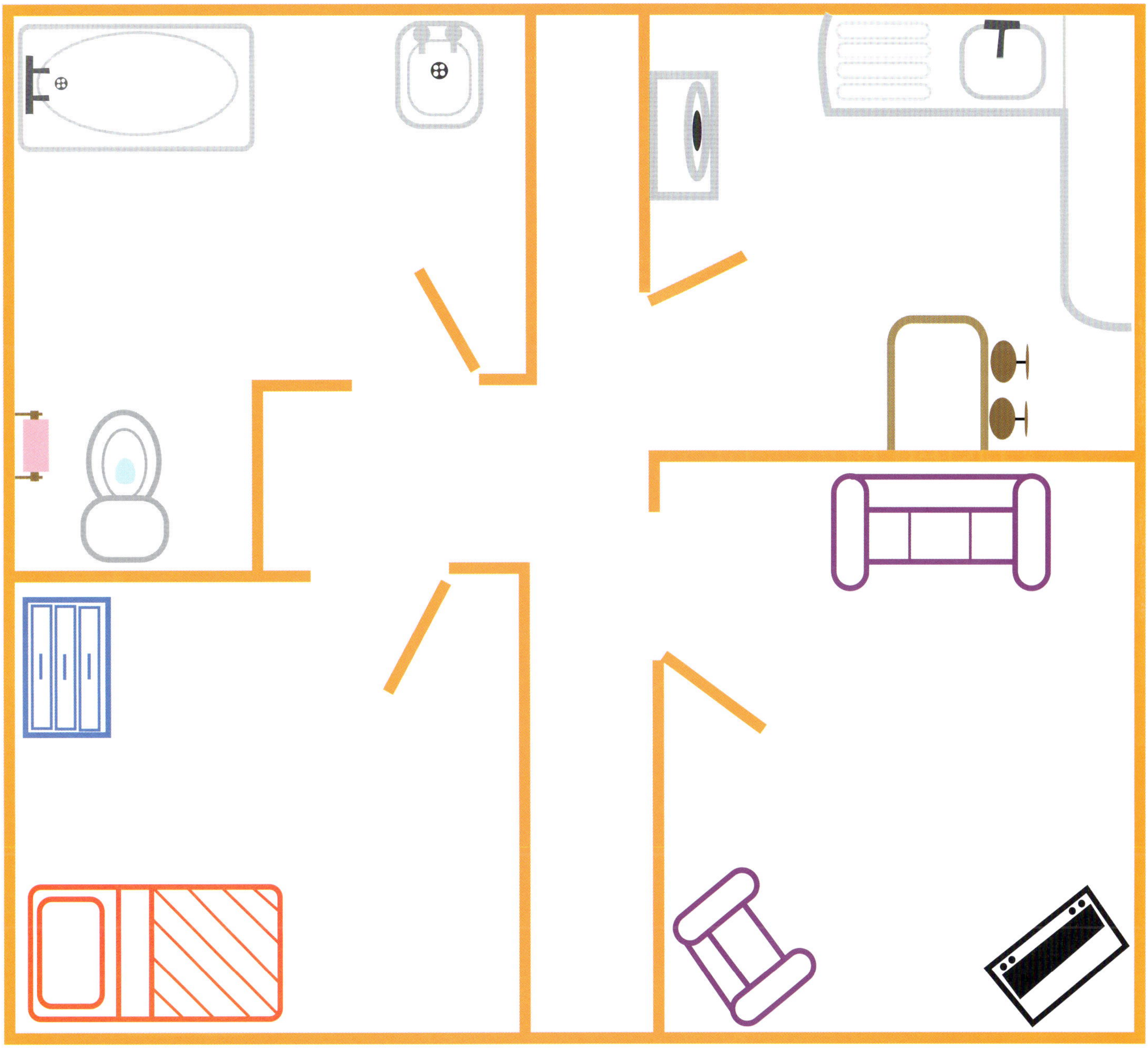

2 Draw and say.

Workbook page 78

Lesson 4

Track 50

1 Listen and point.

Track 51

2 Sing and act out.

Workbook page 79

My Picture Dictionary page 110

Grammar There's a (bed) in the (bedroom).

Track 52

1 Listen and point.

Track 53

2 Listen and circle.

Workbook page 80

1 Circle and say.

2 Tell a friend.

Workbook page 81

Story Time

Track 54

1 Listen and point.

2 Act out.

3 Circle the value.

Love your home.

Workbook page 82

Craft Time

1 Make a house.

2 Show and say.

Workbook page 93

Progress Check

1 Say and color.

Track 55

2 Listen and number.

My Picture Dictionary

Units 1–2

Units 3–4

Units 5–6

Units 7–8

Units 9–10

1 2 3 4 5 6 7 8 9 10

Macmillan Education
4 Crinan Street
London N1 9XW
A division of Springer Nature Limited
Companies and representatives throughout the world

ISBN 978-0-230-44095-1

This edition published by arrangement with Springer Nature, S.A. de C.V.

This edition published 2013
First edition entitled "Next Stop" published 2009 by Springer Nature, S.A. de C.V.

Concept design by Springer Nature Limited, Ben Cracknell Studios, and Deb Oatley at room9design
Page make-up by Mo Choy Design Limited and Deb Oatley at room9design
Icons by Andrew Painter
Illustrated by Chris Embleton (Advocate Art) pp5, 6, 7, 14, 20, 24, 30, 34, 41, 44, 54, 59, 64, 66, 70, 71, 74, 79, 84, 94, 104; Mike Gelen, Inkwell Studios pp9, 20, 28, 37, 40, 49, 60, 61, 68, 76, 77, 80, 90, 91, 100, 101; Bill Ledger pp8, 10, 11, 16, 17, 18, 26, 29, 36, 38, 50, 56, 58, 71, 78, 81, 88, 98, 99; Ed Myer (Advocate Art) pp12, 22, 27, 32, 42, 46, 47, 48, 51, 52, 57, 62, 67, 72, 82, 87, 89, 92, 96, 97, 102, 105, 106, 107, 108, 109, 110; Andrew Painter p4; Joseph Wilkins pp19, 31, 39, 69, 86
Cover design by Springer Nature Limited
Cover illustration by Pablo Scapinachis – Arquiplay
Cover photography by Alamy/Woodbridge Aviation Images (plane), Studio8 (child)
Picture research by Emily Taylor

The authors and publishers would like to thank the following for permission to reproduce their photographs:
Alamy/Brian Elliott p35, Alamy/Tracy Hebden p15; **Corbis**/Theo Allofs p25, Corbis/NASA p5; **Getty Images**/Alan Copson p95, Getty Images/Stuart Dee p85, Getty Images/Christian Heinrich p65, Getty Images/Lew Robertson p75; **Rex Features**/Erik Pendzich p45; **Thinkstock**/iStock/DragonImages p55.

Commissioned photography by Studio8 pp7,8, 13,18, 20, 23, 30, 33, 38, 43, 48, 51, 53, 58, 61, 63, 68, 73, 78, 83, 88, 93,103 .

Printed and bound in Spain

2021 2020 2019 2018
23 22 21 20 19 18 17 16